WOMEN in POLITICS

By Rebecca Phillips-Bartlett

Minneapolis, Minnesota

Credits
All images are courtesy of Shutterstock.com, unless otherwise specified. With thanks to Getty Images, Thinkstock Photo, and iStockphoto. Cover – Amma Shams, balabolka. Throughout – Amma Shams. 4–5 – Ground Picture. 6–7 – mareandmare, HassanEL-gendy. 8–9 – Achille Devéria, Public domain, via Wikimedia Commons, Public Domain, via Wikimedia Commons, UNESCO, CC BY-SA 3.0 <https://creativecommons.org/licenses/by-sa/3.0>, via Wikimedia Commons, Polina Tomtosova. 10–11 – Everett Collection, Rebellion Works. 12–13 – the lost gallery, CC BY 2.0 <https://creativecommons.org/licenses/by/2.0>, via Wikimedia Commons, AKSHAY1234, Moriz, VKA, hudhud94. 14–15 – Public domain, via Wikimedia Commons, Dotidrop. 16–17 – Photographer: Horatio Seymour Squyer, 1848 – 18 Dec 1905, Public domain, via Wikimedia Commons, George J, mimin doodle, Brian Logan Photography. 18–19 – Public domain, via Wikimedia Commons, The Visibility Project, Claudette Colvin, Public domain, via Wikimedia Commons, SunnyColoring, MarSTay, Devita ayu silvianingtyas, ameer_stockphoto, Irina Voziyan. 20–21 – neftali, Cmcmcm1, CC BY-SA 4.0 <https://creativecommons.org/licenses/by-sa/4.0>, via Wikimedia Commons, Devita ayu silvianingtyas, Inga Maya. 22–23 – Rob Crandall, Jay Yuan, Irina Voziyan. 24–25 – Tinseltown, balabolka. 26–27 – Antonello Marangi, Per Grunditz, Olive Kitt, Receh Lancar Jaya, Jane Kelly. 28–29 – Charles Hamilton Smith, Public domain, via Wikimedia Commons, Overlooked: Qiu Jin (only image), Public domain, via Wikimedia Commons, Kingkongphoto & www.celebrity-photos.com from Laurel Maryland, USA, CC BY-SA 2.0 <https://creativecommons.org/licenses/by-sa/2.0>, via Wikimedia Commons, Daniel Hernandez-Salazar, lineartestpilot.

Bearport Publishing Company Product Development Team
President: Jen Jenson; Director of Product Development: Spencer Brinker; Managing Editor: Allison Juda; Associate Editor: Naomi Reich; Associate Editor: Tiana Tran; Art Director: Colin O'Dea; Designer: Kim Jones; Designer: Kayla Eggert; Product Development Assistant: Owen Hamlin

Library of Congress Cataloging-in-Publication Data is available at www.loc.gov or upon request from the publisher.

ISBN: 979-8-88916-980-2 (hardcover)
ISBN: 979-8-89232-512-7 (paperback)
ISBN: 979-8-89232-164-8 (ebook)

© 2025 BookLife Publishing
This edition is published by arrangement with BookLife Publishing.

North American adaptations © 2025 Bearport Publishing Company. All rights reserved. No part of this publication may be reproduced in whole or in part, stored in any retrieval system, or transmitted in any form or by any means, electronic, mechanical, photocopying, recording, or otherwise, without written permission from the publisher. Bearport Publishing is a division of Chrysalis Education Group.

For more information, write to Bearport Publishing, 5357 Penn Avenue South, Minneapolis, MN 55419.

Contents

She Who Dares 4
Hatshepsut 6
Njinga Mbandi 8
Lucretia Mott and Elizabeth Cady Stanton .. 10
Lakshmi Bai 12
Emmeline Pankhurst 14
Harriet Tubman 16
Rosa Parks and Claudette Colvin 18
Sophie Scholl 20
Ruth Bader Ginsburg 22
Malala Yousafzai 24
Greta Thunberg 26

More Daring Women 28
Changing the World 30
Glossary 31
Index 32
Read More 32
Learn More Online 32

She Who Dares

Think about the rules you follow every day. Who made those rules? How might they help you or others do the right thing?

From the rules in a classroom to the laws of a country, people all over the world have rules to follow. Over time, people realize some rules need to change to make them more fair. However, change doesn't just happen overnight! Countless women in politics have dared to stand up for what they believe in and lead the charge for change.

> Many women in politics use **activism** to make their voices heard. They hold protests, write powerful speeches, and create art to spread their messages.

LADIES WHO LEAD

Throughout history, many women were not able to become leaders or even vote for the people in charge. Today, women in many countries have those rights, but it took a lot of hard work to make that happen.

Plenty of daring women have had to break through **barriers** to become leaders and changemakers. They found strength in their determination to make a difference for themselves and others.

Standing up for what you believe takes lots of bravery and courage.

What helps you when you are facing a big challenge?

Hatshepsut

A PHENOMENAL PHARAOH

 Born: Around 1508 BCE   **Died:** Around 1458 BCE

Hatshepsut was born in ancient Egypt. Her father was the king, but this did not mean she would become the next ruler. That powerful title was usually passed down to the king's oldest son. So, Hatshepsut's brother became king.

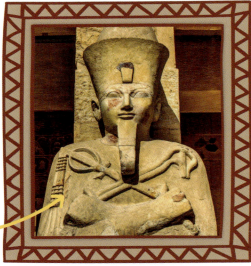

A statue of Hatshepsut

After a few years as king, Hatshepsut's brother died. His only son was just a baby, so he couldn't rule. Hatshepsut stepped up to help rule while the child grew up. Even though she didn't have the title of king, she did all of the work.

Hatshepsut was a very popular leader. Soon, she rose above her title as co-ruler and became a **pharaoh**. She was one of the few female pharaohs in the history of ancient Egypt!

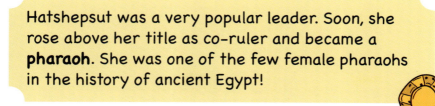

During her rule, Hatshepsut oversaw the creation of many buildings, temples, and gardens. She helped bring more trade to ancient Egypt. Hatshepsut ruled for more than 20 years and is remembered as one of Egypt's most successful pharaohs.

Many statues of Hatshepsut show her with a fake beard. This was meant to show that she was just as powerful as male rulers.

Njinga Mbandi

NOBLE NEGOTIATOR

Born: Around 1581   **Died:** 1663

Njinga Mbandi was born into the royal family of the Ndongo kingdom in Central Africa. At the time, Portuguese armies were trying to take control of the kingdom's land and rule over the people who lived there.

When Mbandi's father died, her brother became king and attacks from the Portuguese increased. Mbandi was great at talking with people, so she stepped in to help her brother. She met with the Portuguese leaders and **negotiated** an agreement that they would leave the Ndongo kingdom alone.

It is said that the Portuguese leaders did not give Mbandi a chair when they met. They wanted to make her feel inferior. So, instead Mbandi sat on the back of a loyal worker.

8

When her brother died a few years later, Mbandi became queen. But before long, Portugal broke its agreement and began attacking Ndongo once again. Mbandi bravely led her people farther west to avoid the Portuguese armies. There, she set up the new kingdom of Matamba.

Mbandi did all she could to protect her people, and Matamba became very powerful. She set up an army and found ways for the people of her kingdom to earn money. She even created safe places for other African people who had run away from the Portuguese.

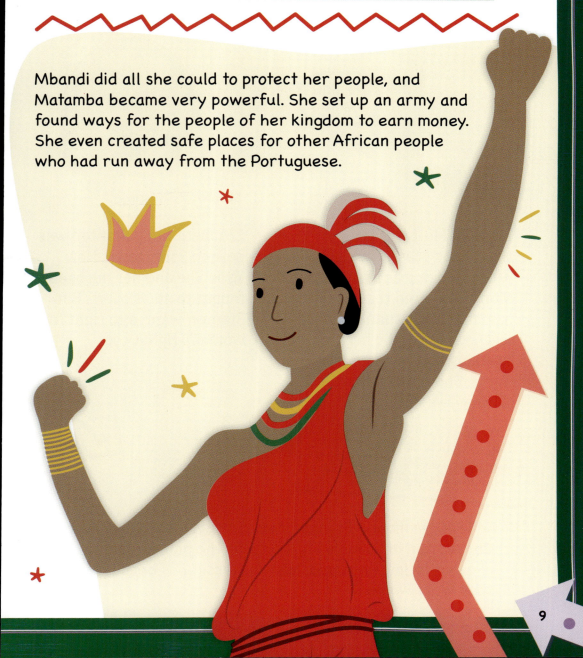

Lucretia Mott and Elizabeth Cady Stanton

SISTERS FOR SUFFRAGE

Born: 1793   **Died:** 1880

Born: 1815   **Died:** 1902

Lucretia Mott

Elizabeth Cady Stanton

Lucretia Mott was born in Nantucket, Massachusetts. While working as a teacher, Mott discovered that she was paid much less than the male teachers. Soon, she began speaking about women's rights. She spoke out against slavery, too.

Elizabeth Cady Stanton was born in Johnstown, New York. She and her husband fought to end slavery. But Stanton wanted to fight for women's rights, too.

Many people criticized Mott because they believed women shouldn't be public speakers.

In 1840, Mott and Stanton met at the World Anti-Slavery **Convention** in London, England. But the pair were not allowed to join any important conversations because they were women.

10

Mott and Stanton didn't want to just watch while men got to have their voices heard. They decided to hold an event all about women's rights once they were back in the United States.

In 1848, Mott and Stanton held a meeting called the Seneca Falls Convention. They made speeches supporting women's rights, including the right to vote. This event was the beginning of the long fight for women's **suffrage** in the United States. Mott and Stanton continued fighting. Finally, by August 1920, many women across the country had gained the right to vote!

Every year, the United States celebrates Women's Equality day on August 26. It falls on the anniversary of the day women gained the right to vote.

Lakshmi Bai

FIGHTER FOR FREEDOM

Born: Around 1835   **Died:** 1858

Lakshmi Bai was born in Varanasi, India. Her family was very rich, so she learned important skills that were usually taught only to boys. She studied archery, horseback riding, and self-defense.

Lakshmi Bai's home

Bai married the **maharaja** of Jhansi, India. Just before her husband died, the couple adopted a son who would become maharaja once he was older. In the meantime, Bai handled the responsibilities of ruling Jhansi. But the British armies did not accept her or the adopted son as rulers. They ordered her to leave her home, but Bai was determined not to give up.

12

In 1857, a huge **rebellion** broke out in India. People across the country were fighting for their freedom from the British.

In order to protect her people, Bai decided that Jhansi would join the rebellion. She bravely led her army into the fight for freedom. Although she died during battle, Bai is remembered as a **martyr**, a freedom fighter, and one of India's greatest warriors.

Rebels from other places in India headed to Jhansi to offer Bai their support.

Bai has inspired people to stand up for their freedom. Many poems have been written about her. Schools and ships have been named after her, too.

Emmeline Pankhurst

POWERFUL PROTESTER

Born: 1858   **Died:** 1928

Emmeline Pankhurst was born into a very politically active family in Manchester, England. She was just 14 years old when she attended her first women's suffrage meeting.

In 1903, Pankhurst decided that it was time to do something more than just speak about women's rights. She set up a group called the Women's Social and Political Union (WSPU). The WSPU held protests and often used violent methods, such as smashing windows and starting fires, to make their voices heard.

Pankhurst was arrested several times for protesting.

Many WSPU members were arrested in the fight for their rights. The women continued to protest while in prison. However, when World War I (1914–1918) began, Pankhurst decided the WSPU should shift its focus to helping with the war effort.

Women across the country took on important jobs, such as driving buses and working in factories. Once the war was over, the WSPU turned its attention back to the cause. In July 1928, just a few weeks after Pankhurst died, women in the United Kingdom gained equal voting rights.

Deeds Not Words

The WSPU's **motto** was Deeds Not Words. They used actions, or deeds, to prove why women should have the right to vote.

VOTES for WOMEN

Harriet Tubman

FEARLESS PATHFINDER

Born: Around 1820   **Died:** 1913

Harriet Tubman was born in Dorchester County, Maryland. Her parents were **enslaved** people and were forced to work for a rich landowner.

When Tubman was 12 years old, the landowner got very angry and threw a heavy weight at one of the enslaved workers. Tubman could not sit by and watch. She jumped in front of the man and the weight hit her in the head. For the rest of her life, she suffered from very bad headaches. She also developed narcolepsy, a condition that caused her to fall asleep at unexpected times.

In 1849, Tubman managed to escape. She was helped by the Underground Railroad. This network of secret paths, safe houses, and **abolitionists** helped enslaved people get to the north. Tubman had to travel almost 90 miles (145 km) to freedom.

But Tubman could not be happy while her family was still suffering. So, she joined the Underground Railroad. She bravely traveled back to her family and led them to freedom, too. But Tubman wasn't finished. She returned many times to help dozens of others escape slavery.

Statue of Tubman leading others to freedom

During the U.S. Civil War (1861–1865), Tubman worked as a nurse and a spy for the Union Army.

Rosa Parks and Claudette Colvin

BEGINNING THE BUS BOYCOTTS

Born: 1913   **Died:** 2005

Born: 1939

Rosa Parks was born in Tuskegee, Alabama. She grew up under strict **segregation** laws. These laws kept people of color separate from White people.

Claudette Colvin grew up in Montgomery, Alabama. At her segregated school, she learned about Black activists, such as Harriet Tubman. They inspired her to fight for her rights.

In 1943, Parks joined the National Association for the Advancement of Colored People (NAACP). The NAACP worked to end segregation and give Black people equal rights.

In March 1955, Colvin was riding the bus home from school when the driver told her and other Black riders to move for a White passenger. She refused.

Because of Alabama's segregation laws, Black people had to go to separate schools and sit in separate sections on the bus from White people.

Colvin was pulled off the bus and arrested. Just nine months later, Parks had a similar experience. She was arrested for not moving for a White passenger.

Parks' arrest got lots of attention. The NAACP used it to start a bus **boycott.** Black people stopped using buses. This means, the buses stopped getting their money, too. The boycott lasted a whole year.

During the boycott, Colvin appeared in court to argue against bus segregation. Colvin, Parks, and the many other activists helped to end bus segregation in the United States.

Boycotts are still a powerful way to show you do not agree with something. Have you ever stopped using something in order to send a message?

Sophie Scholl

ANTI-NAZI ACTIVIST

  Born: 1921 **Died:** 1943

Sophie Scholl was born in Forchtenberg, Germany. She was proud of her country. Then, in 1933, the Nazi party came into power. During the next few years, they kidnapped and took belongings from Jews and others. The Nazis began killing millions.

The White Rose memorial in Munich, Germany

In 1942, Scholl's brother and his friends started an anti-Nazi group called the White Rose. Sophie Scholl was the only woman to join. She was a very valuable member since women were less likely to be stopped and searched by the police. This allowed her to secretly hand out anti-Nazi **leaflets**.

In February 1943, Scholl threw hundreds of leaflets into a busy hall at her college. Unfortunately, she was caught. Scholl and many other members of the White Rose were immediately arrested.

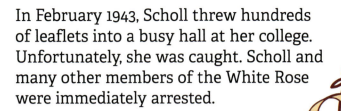

Scholl threw leaflets into this hall.

Even in court, Scholl spoke out for what she believed. She was found guilty of treason and was executed when she was just 21 years old. Today, Scholl's bravery and determination is celebrated throughout Germany.

Sophie Scholl, her brother, and the other members of the White Rose are honored to this day. Many schools, roads, and awards are named after them.

Ruth Bader Ginsburg

LADY OF THE LAW

Born: 1933   **Died:** 2020

Ruth Bader Ginsburg was born in Brooklyn, New York. Growing up, she loved learning. She studied very hard and went to a great college.

Soon after graduating, Ginsburg got married and had a baby. While raising her child, she went to Harvard Law School. At the time, there were only 9 women in her class of 500 students. Ginsburg changed schools and finished her education at Columbia Law School. She graduated at the top of her class and became a lawyer.

Ginsburg faced lots of **discrimination** for being a woman, including not being allowed in certain parts of the library.

In 1972, Ginsburg helped start a group called the Women's Rights Project. The group worked to ensure women had equal rights under the law. Ginsburg often went before the U.S. Supreme Court to argue important cases on gender equality.

The Supreme Court is the highest court in the United States. It has the power to strike down laws and change decisions made by lower courts.

By 1993, Ginsburg became a judge on the Supreme Court. She used her position to **advocate** for workers' rights, women's rights, and equality for all people.

Ginsburg was the second woman and the first Jewish woman to serve on the U.S. Supreme Court.

Malala Yousafzai

EDUCATION ADVOCATE

Born: 1997

Malala Yousafzai was born in Mingora, Pakistan. Growing up, she studied at a school that her father started. By the time she was 10 years old, a group called the Taliban had taken control of the area. The Taliban did not believe women should be allowed to learn and tried to close all the girls' schools.

Yousafzai started writing a blog about life under Taliban control. She spoke out against the changes that were happening in her country. Although she wrote under a fake name, the Taliban found out it was her and began threatening her.

When Yousafzai was 15 years old, a member of the Taliban boarded her school bus and shot her. She was very badly injured and was rushed to a hospital in England. Once she was better, Yousafzai continued her education in England.

On her 16th birthday, Yousafzai gave a speech at the United Nations, advocating for women's right to education. At 17 years old, she became the youngest person to win a Nobel Peace Prize.

In 2011, Yousafzai won Pakistan's National Youth Peace Prize.

July 12th is Malala Day. This day celebrates the work that Yousafzai has done to fight for all children's rights to education.

Greta Thunberg

PROTECTOR OF THE PLANET

Born: 2003

Greta Thunberg was born in Stockholm, Sweden. At the age of eight, she started learning about climate change. She wondered why so little was being done to help the planet. So, Thunberg began making changes in her own life, such as not flying on airplanes.

Thunberg has **autism** and believes it helps her see the issues of climate change very clearly.

When Thunberg was 15 years old, she took further action. Instead of going to school, she sat outside Swedish **parliament** holding a sign that read "School Strike for Climate." She wanted the politicians to see how important climate issues are.

A strike is a type of protest where people do not go to work or school to show that they want something to change.

Thunberg continued her school strikes each Friday, attracting lots of attention as time went on. Soon, students around the world were joining the strikes that Thunberg called Fridays for Future.

Now, Thunberg travels the world, sharing the importance of protecting the planet. Wherever she goes, Thunberg makes sure to find a climate-friendly way to get there. In 2019, she traveled for two weeks on a boat to get to the United Nations Climate Action Summit in New York.

While in New York, Thunberg was part of the largest climate protest in history. That day, four million people took a stand against climate change.

In 2019, Thunberg became the youngest person to be named *Time* magazine's Person of the Year.

More Daring Women

BOUDICA and Her Bravery in Battle

Born: Around 30 CE **Died:** Around 61 CE

Boudica was queen of the Iceni tribe in England. When her husband died, Roman armies stole his land and forced the tribe to leave. Boudica raised an army and led a revolt against the Roman forces.

Today, Boudica is celebrated as a national hero of England.

QIU JIN and Her Powerful Poetry

Born: 1875 **Died:** 1907

Qiu Jin is remembered as a hero in China.

Qiu Jin was a poet from eastern China. Many of her poems were about female heroes and warriors from Chinese history. She celebrated their bravery and strength. Qiu also used her poetry to speak out against systems that did not treat women well. When her words failed, she went on to train warriors to fight.

WANGARI MAATHAI and Her Fight Against Deforestation

Born: 1940   **Died:** 2011

Wangari Maathai lived in Kenya. In 1977, she started the Green Belt Movement. This movement encourages women to plant trees to help stop **deforestation**. To date, they have planted more than 51 million trees!

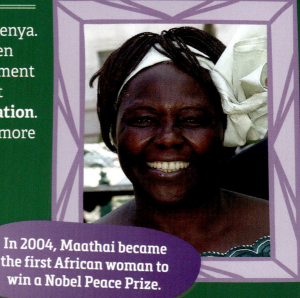

In 2004, Maathai became the first African woman to win a Nobel Peace Prize.

KAMALA HARRIS and Her Political Power

Born: 1964

Kamala Harris was born in Oakland, California. Politics has always been a part of her life. When she was a baby, her mother took her to civil rights marches. In 2021, Harris became the vice president of the United States.

Harris is the first woman and the first Black American and Indian American person to become vice president of the United States.

Changing the World

Many women have worked hard to make the world a better place. Whether they were standing up to unfair laws, fighting to protect their people, or teaching others to protect the planet, the world would not be the same without women in politics!

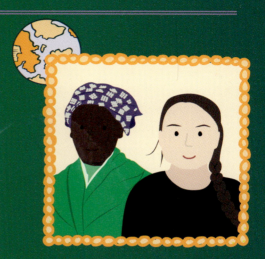

Making a difference is not always easy. These women had the bravery and strength to break through barriers that stood in their way. They dared to be different so they could change the world.

What issue do you care about? How can you take action to help make a difference?

DO YOU DARE TO CHANGE THE WORLD?

 # Glossary

abolitionists people who worked to end slavery

activism a practice that encourages support and action toward change

advocate to support or speak in favor of something

autism a condition that makes the brain function in a different way, sometimes making social interactions challenging

barriers obstacles that block or limit access to something

boycott to refuse to buy or use something in order to protest

convention a meeting of people to work toward a common goal

deforestation the clearing or loss of trees

discrimination the unfair treatment of people because of a certain trait

enslaved made to be a person who is owned by others and is forced to do hard work without pay

leaflets sheets of paper that give information about something

maharaja a Hindu prince

martyr a person who is killed because of their beliefs

motto a saying that states what someone believes in

negotiated reached an agreement by talking or making a deal

parliament a group of people who have been elected to make laws in some countries

pharaoh a ruler in ancient Egypt

rebellion an effort by many people to change the leader and rules of a place, often by force

segregation a forced separation of people, often by race

suffrage the right to vote

INDEX

armies 8–9, 12–13, 17, 28
Boudica 28
boycotts 18–19
climate change 26–27
Colvin, Claudette 18–19
Ginsburg, Ruth Bader 22–23
Harris, Kamala 29
Hatshepsut 6–7
laws 18, 22–23, 30
Maathai, Wangari 29
Mbandi, Njinga 8–9
Mott, Lucretia 10–11
Nobel Peace Prize 25, 29
Pankhurst, Emmeline 14–15
Parks, Rosa 18–19
poems 13, 28
protests 4, 14–15, 26–27
Qiu, Jin 28
Scholl, Sophie 20–21
schools 13, 18, 21–22, 24–27
Stanton, Elizabeth Cady 10–11
suffrage 10–11, 14
Thunberg, Greta 26–27
Tubman, Harriet 16–18
votes 5, 11, 15
warriors 13, 28
Yousafzai, Malala 24–25

READ MORE

Rolka, Gail Meyer. *100 Women Who Shaped World History (100 Series).* Naperville, IL: Sourcebooks Explore, 2022.

Sarah, Rachel. *Girl Warriors: How 25 Young Activists Are Saving the Earth.* Chicago: Chicago Review Press, 2021.

Sher, Abby. *Climate Warriors: 25 Tales of Women Who Protect the Earth (Rebel Girls).* Mankato, MN: Black Rabbit Books, 2023.

LEARN MORE ONLINE

1. Go to **www.factsurfer.com** or scan the QR code below.
2. Enter **"Women in Politics"** into the search box.
3. Click on the cover of this book to see a list of websites.